T0171512

50
POEMS
NOW

By Sandra Sanders

Order this book online at www.trafford.com
or email orders@trafford.com

Most Trafford titles are also available at major online book retailers.

Note for Librarians: A cataloguing record for this book is available from Library
and Archives Canada at www.collectionscanada.ca/amicus/index-e.html

Printed in Victoria, BC, Canada.

ISBN: 978-1-4269-0323-6 (Soft)

*We at Trafford believe that it is the responsibility of us all, as both individuals
and corporations, to make choices that are environmentally and socially sound.
You, in turn, are supporting this responsible conduct each time you purchase a
Trafford book, or make use of our publishing services. To find out how you are
helping, please visit www.trafford.com/responsiblepublishing.html*

*Our mission is to efficiently provide the world's finest, most comprehensive
book publishing service, enabling every author to experience success.
To find out how to publish your book, your way, and have it available
worldwide, visit us online at www.trafford.com*

Trafford rev. 6/12/2009

 www.trafford.com

North America & international
toll-free: 1 888 232 4444 (USA & Canada)
phone: 250 383 6864 ✦ fax: 250 383 6804 ✦ email: info@trafford.com

The United Kingdom & Europe
phone: +44 (0)1865 487 395 ✦ local rate: 0845 230 9601
facsimile: +44 (0)1865 481 507 ✦ email: info.uk@trafford.com

10 9 8 7 6 5 4 3 2 1

To Nana, who would be proud

—SS

FORWARD

In December of 2008 the author went on a cruise to the Bahamas. Most of the poems in this book were inspired by that cruise.

THE 'IT' MERMAID

With leopard arms
And leopard tail
The 'It' Mermaid
Again sets sail

Her hair, dark blue
At the nape
Then turquoise blue
Hangs like a cape

Born near the shore
Of Lake Champlain,
She left Vermont
With cool disdain

Now she can be seen
By the Mediterranean shore
Sunning freestyle on a rock
Enjoying life so much more

She keeps a gold tower,
A tower of filigree
Adorned with good-luck charms
Displayed for all to see;

Charms given by her visitors
Seeking mermaid blessing,
She welcomes you to leave one too,
For those issues that are pressing—

MYSTERY LADY

Small Philippino lady
Fur coated, at the pier,
Your husband, dark skinned
Stands silent beside you

Toasted almond lady,
Hawaiian lady,
Long, black hair,
Hair full of fluffy body

Movie star lady;
Glamorous gold lame sandals,
Gold-tinted sunglasses,
Large and exotic ones

Classy lady,
Are you from an island?
Or, just Rhode Island?
I cannot tell

Thin-lipped lady,
Chin held high,
Mouth tight,
Your hand taps a melody

Quiet, princess lady,
Your husband picks his teeth,
You gaze straight ahead,
He continues picking

Sun tanned lady,
Diamonds on her hand,
Her sandal glints
By the pool side

Wrinkled lady,
She is not young
But more elegant
Than the young

Gem Cruise lady,
You leave the pool area
In a flowing yellow mu mu;
Stepping royalty

*Seen on an NCL cruise

RED ROSE TEA

How the English love their tea
They sip and serve it elegantly—

Is it P G Tips
That they touch to their lips?

It is not, I must say,
It is not, in any way

They steep the best, that's the thing,
They steep the tea with the most bling

Tea with a red rose on each label
Come and see, if you are able

Red Rose Tea is the choice
With a biscuit, come add your voice

Red Rose Tea, have a taste
Before it cools and do make haste!

How the English love their tea
They serve and sip it elegantly—

GARAM MASALA

Put it in your food

For a taste

That you will see

Is so very good—

For bread, we'll have naan

And we will use

A tandoor

For a pan—

THE FLYING FISH

I found it on deck seven lying on white sheet metal
Its mouth open in a little circle
With a forked tail and narrow, cellophane wings
Pinned to fishy sides—

A fish of silver and blue-gray,
It was quite stiff for it had died a stow-away
Cast in by the tide; blown in by the wind;
The twelve foot high waves that night—

Only about ten inches long,
Like a large sardine
Or a pretty blue butterfly whose song was over,
It would never skim or sail waters again…

But, this offering from the sea
This special thing of mystery
That flew in on the glistening wind
Was given just to me—

EDELSTEIN-DET HAVFRUE*

The 'It' Mermaid was seen again…
This time wrapped in her leopard shawl or cape,
She stole the show when she appeared;
They got it all down on tape—

They cordoned off her beach
While she waved all the time and smiled;
They kept back the milling crowd,
For she had them quite beguiled—

*Norwegian for: Gem-It Mermaid

ETOILES DE NUIT*

The sky was black-blue with only two stars showing,

That was because the storm clouds were blowing...

When the moon came out, what a sight there be*

For the waves, shiny white, were churning up the sea...

*French for: Stars of the Night
*Intentionally incorrect grammar

DIE SEEJUNGFRAU*

The 'It' Mermaid smiles a lot
When she collects a charm,
Her jewelry, her favorite thing,
She wears on neck and arm…

A marcasite starfish on her forehead
Parts blue-turquoise hair;
A gold circle and spotted pendant
Rest on her chest so bare

She loves to hear you are afraid
Of what she can do
If displeased by a ship;
Its passengers or crew…

She loves to hear she'll brew a storm
Or make the seas quite rough;
That she'll do it very soon
If you don't give her enough

Her likeness-doll is by the bridge
She hopes you take a look,
Then, all that you need do
Is open your pocketbook…

*German for: The Mermaid

THE SHIP COUNTER

I sat on a rock in Langelinie Bay
To spot the big cruise ships
That traveled up that way…

I saw the Majesty, Dream, Spirit, Sun—
I shifted on my frozen hips
And counted every one…

I saw the Star, Dawn, Jewel, Pearl—
I counted with my stiffened lips
And gave my tail a curl…

I saw the Jade, Gem, Pride, Sky—
Not all in Langelinie slips
But, they did go passing by…

*All ships mentioned are NCL ships

COCONUT WIND CHIME

A gentle sound emanated
Above my head,
A flute-like melody
Mellow as a reed
Speaking in different pitches
Of the islands;
The sun—
Nassau—
I looked up,
A half coconut hung there
With hollow bamboo stems;
Colorful fishes painted on them
It spoke warmly;
Tubes tapping each other
Above my head

BOURBON CREAMS

Oh, those Jacob's cookies,

Those chocolate Bourbon Creams—

They make them in Ireland;

The cookie of my dreams—

*Purchased in Nassau

ON THE BRIDGE OF THE GEM

She sits on leopard tail in the bridge room,
That clean room with three large consoles;
An ocean view,
Some Danish on a tray,
Cigarettes too…

She speaks to the captain
Murmuring in mermaidese,
Much pleased
To see her display on deck eleven
The bridge viewing room;
A piece of heaven…

She takes all the gems she wants to wear,
Returning others, she deposits them there
She laughs and tosses her blue hair grand
While the captain stands up
To shake her lovely, long hand…

THE CHARM COLLECTION

A little ball
A prism
An apple
A globe
A seahorse
A yin-yang
A strawberry
A leopard heart
A pear
AND MORE ARE THERE!

A tower
An angel
A Statue of Liberty
A 'welcome home'
A fish tail
An anchor
Three dolphins
An eagle
A cross
The state of Minnesota
THERE'S NO END TO THE QUOTA!

LA PETITE SIRENE

One night I fell asleep
And I had a dream
I dreamt I lived far away;
I was 'La Petite Sirene'

From my river home
I saw the Eiffel Tower,
It was all lit up that night
Like a glowing water flower

*French for: The Little Mermaid

ATHOL ISLAND

When the sky is sullen gray
And the high winds blow
I think of the place
Where I want to go,

There to Athol Island
Is where I want to be
Spotting spotted fishes
Swimming in the sea,

Where brown stag and elk horn coral rises,
And sea fans wave 'hello'
Brain coral grows in the garden
Just five feet down below,

Where spotlight parrotfish
At a tall, vase-like bowl
Slurp down some pea soup
At the great atoll—

*Athol Island, Nassau, Grand Bahamas

ANTARCTICA

The ice floe is still,
Low and melted looking,
Whorled like soft, vanilla ice cream
But, light blue close up,
The floe behind is whiter
It fades to gray where the water touches it;
The deep, strong-blue water,
Calm, with a hint of green in it,
Which supports them...
No sun is out,
Instead, swirls of pale amber-tan clouds
Close in on the ice floe
Enveloping it in a quiet fog...

CHANUKAH LIGHTS

M accabees

E lephants

N un

O il

R uler Antiochus IV

A pplesauce

H ogs

SUFGANIOT

Little jelly doughnuts
Full of jam inside,
To taste one is heaven
In Israel they're fried—

Brown and dark outside
Pale and white within,
Apricot or purple jam
Drips down on the chin—

On this Chanukah
We'll fly to Israel,
Sufganiot, they have a lot
And we will eat our fill—

*Sufganiot: SOO - FAH - **NYOHT**

LA SIRENITA*

Mermaid in the lake
Seen by the pregnant lady,
Alas! Too late to flee
The damage done her baby!

A baby to be born
With legs fused together
Wrapped in a coating of tight skin;
Moving like a lever—

The mother went to the lake
To reverse the charm,
Alas! The mermaid did not show
To undo the syndrome's harm—

*La Sirenita: Spanish for 'The Mermaid'
*Sirenomelia: A rare genetic defect, usually fatal, giving one
the appearance of a mermaid

BUCKAROO

Buckaroo's an appaloosa;
Big spots on every inch,
Dark brown, they are so loud
They'll make you want to flinch—

His tail is white at the top
And yellow at the end,
Such a pretty horse
You'll want him for a friend—

Once, a rodeo horse,
He is retired now
No more bucking for buckaroo
That is his solemn vow!

SOUVENIRS

I see them a lot
Those Danish souvenirs,
Those bronze half-mermaids
Sitting in the air—
Some, sunbathing on the rock
Some searching the passing ships
Longing to see the prince
Who doesn't know and doesn't care—

Black are the older ones,
Copper-colored, the younger;
Always on their native rocks
Viewing the harbor there—
The rocks say 'Kobenhavn' or 'Danmark'
With little red and white flags
Pasted down on them
By the fins of the ladies who stare—

*The souvenirs are not in the same position as the original
mermaid in the bay because she is copyrighted

BETHELEHEM

I put my star over all the earth
To announce the Messiah's birth—

I placed my star there for all to see
That from death they could be free—*

I am the Morning Star,
Yeshua, is my name*

I am the Son of God,
The Holy One who came—

*death: The spiritual death inherited from Adam and Eve
*Yeshua: Hebrew for 'Salvation'

DOWN IN THE DEPTHS

In the depths of the sea
Close to the bottom
The water is blue—
Curious and rare

Where it's all blue,
Even the shelves
That rise there—
Curious and rare

The plants and the corals
Moored together
Wave bluely—
Curious and rare

The little mermaids
Sit on the ledges
Reaching out—
Curious and rare

Little moons in their hair,
Sparkling crescents
In the blue light—
Curious and rare

Their faces are hidden
In the blue shadows;
The blue streaks of the sea—
Curious and rare

Down in the chalky depths
Of mute turquoise
And glowing algae—
Curious and rare

LILLE HAVFRUE*

Brown hair floating up
She puts her hands to it,
Stretching lithely, arching her back—
Swirling brown hair in the current,
She closes her eyes
Daring to dream of what lies above the waters—

Her long tail, a rusty color
Reflecting all the blues, greens and gray of the sea
Is surrounded by a legion of dragon seahorses
Where it touches the bottom limestone—
The end is pale gray
It has the required oysters attached
The oysters of royalty—

A princess, she will make a debut
To a new world,
One she only imagines now
With a pounding heart,
Closed eyes—

*Danish: Little Mermaid

PERKY BUNNIES

Orange grass
Ochre flowers on brown stems
Bright orange hearts
A pink heart — one!

Two little black bunnies leap
And spring in a soft white patch,
Dark eyes flashing
Hours of — fun!

A little boy at the resort colors
With crayons flying
Colors a picture,
The bunnies that — run!

*Pocmont Resort

THE GREAT GALLEON

She watched from a rock,
Leaning against it
Near the pier
In the fog—

The great, tall, wooden ship;
Rows of windows lit
Under the crescent moon
In the fog—

Two rows of black windows
Three rows of lit
Some with diamond-panes
In the fog—

The tall sails billowed softly
Hardly a whisper
Beneath, the flags hung quietly
In the fog—

The water, so still
Rippled like gray glass
As the ship slipped past
In the fog—

The ship was leaving
Quietly, it was slipping away
The mermaid made a decision
In the fog—

She would follow it
This curious thing of wonder
She would fathom it
In the fog—

*Galleon: a heavy square-rigged sailing ship of the15th to early 18th centuries used for war or commerce

WHAT IS IT LIKE?

What is it like to wake up at sea
To stretch out the arms and curl the tail,
To yawn underwater
And then exhale?

To be cool in the water,
As cool as a fish
And to rise from your bed
With a squiggly swish?

THE GRAY SEAL

The seal's front half was dull gray
His back half, dirty-gold
Covered with matted hair,
Dead hair that was old—

The seal sniffed at the tea-colored water
As he rested on the shore
By the Delaware river
Where seals haven't been seen before—

So, a rescuer came by to rescue him
But, he protested, barking loudly
And avoiding the net
Swam away rather proudly—

THE HAREM MASTER

The male seals clash together
Neck to huge neck
Both stretched up high,
Up to the sky—

One, with head tossed back
Both, with mouths wide open
Under bulbous snouts,
Threatening pouts—

The intruder came too close to the females
Of the harem master;
Those small seals resting on the sand
Where seagulls, quiet stand—

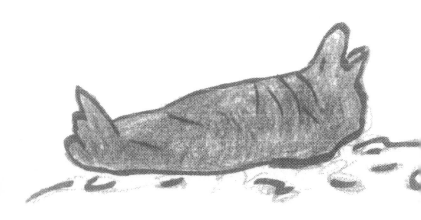

THE CRUISE

Bon voyage, luv!

Bon voyage, I say

Hope you have a very good day

Hope you love wherever you stay

Bon voyage, luv

Bon voyage today!

THE MEADOWSWEET

What a treat it is to meet
An army of marching meadowsweet

They brandish their piked, pink flower ream
Above serrated banners of dusty green

Sky pilot, rain your lemon-light
So their steeples will glow fuzzy and white

Marbled butterfly, come kiss a spire
Of mini apple blooms, wholesome, entire

Snatch about, you bandy gnats
Dunk in sunlight with silent 'snaps'

Listen to the meadow sweet go
'Plink', 'Plink', 'Plink', —just so

Come and listen to the crushing beat
Of this multi-mini meadowsweet

*Written in College

LADYLAKE

In a lake
In a park
He saw her head,
A head above the water;
A head which moved through the water,
A woman in the lake!
He wondered where she would swim
Which shore she would embark
But she dived beneath
With a hint of dark green following
Then a glint of yellow-green—
He watched and waited
For her to resurface
But she didn't…
Alarmed, he notified the park guard;
"A woman has drowned!"
"You saw a duck and nothing more—"
In a lake
In a park

*   *   *

Obsessed, he returned to watch for her
Again and again
Finally, he rented a boat;
A rowboat for fishing
And he rowed out in the evening
And looked into the gray water,
The same water which was frozen and green
And edged with white sheet ice in the winter…

Suddenly, she arose by the boat;
That head again,
With clear, green eyes…
They looked at him steadily,
Made him dizzy—
"Help me!" she said
He heard it distinctly;
"Help me!"
"How?" he stammered
"Take me to the river," she said
His heart melted for her and he agreed to take her—
Then, she drew herself up into the boat
He covered her with a blanket
No one would see—
No one would know—
He drove her away in his car

*   *   *

By the Delaware
He carried her down a steep hill,
Walked out on the wet sand
The tide was in…
She dragged herself into the water
Then she was gliding;
Buoyant—
Shimmering—
Then, sinking down under
She was gone in a flash!
No good-byes
Just some green scales on the pebbles…

He took them home,
Saved them...
Who was she?
What was her name?
He had never asked
But, he often returned—
She never came back
He never saw her again...

*　　*　　*

A few years later
He was seen with his new wife,
A lady with pale green eyes,
Strolling along the same river...

FORSYTHIAS

"YOU!", "YOU!", "YOU!"
The green forsythia branches say—

"YOU!", "YOU!", "YOU!"
They jab and point my way—

"YOU!", "YOU!", "YOU!"
I stand accused this day—

*A dream

GRISWALD

Dwarf Hotots are cute indeed
And Griswald was no exception,
He was a black and white piebald
And not of white complexion

White Dwarf Hotots are the rule
And a piebald rabbit is *out*,
It was a lucky day for Griswald
That I had come about

Griswald couldn't talk
But, he loved me so
He would jump up and down,
Up and down he'd go!

I purchased a doe for him
Jill, was her name,
A gray and white piebald
But, she wasn't quite the same—

*Hotot: **HOE** - TOE; A breed of dwarf rabbit registered
with ARBA

BAROOCH ATAH ADONAI

The beginning of a blessing
These Hebrew words of prayer portray
An honor it is to say them
To do it every day…

"Blessed are you O Lord"
May there never be a parting
From these words of hope and love,
The blessing is now starting!

MERMAID CHILDREN

Two little mermaids
Lay in the sand, on their stomachs
Where the blue water comes rolling in waves
Coating the shoreline with a solid, white foam border
And a lacey foam network where it withdraws again…
They dare each other to stay there…

The smaller child has hands under her chin
Tail curled up and twisted towards the end
She looks to the left…

The other child has one arm stretched in front, one under her chin
Tail raised up straight
She looks to the right…

They ponder the rocky cliffs nearby,
The house far down the beach…
The older child looks up with mild apprehension
A little afraid of the airplane going by…

Then, their mother calls
And chubby cheeks and little chins turn to her
Obediently, they wriggle into the water
Very obediently…

GREAT STIRRUP CAY

S tarfish down below

T enders take you there

U nderwater snorkeling in the cove

R ippling tide pools

R ushing, geyser-like waves breaking

U pon the rocks

P ath to the lighthouse

S ee the Norwegian Gem nearby

*

C oral bedrock

A nd some coconut trees

Y es, we'll come again!

*Originally Sturrup's Cay, Great Stirrup Cay is now the NCL's private island

THE WHITE-CROWNED PIGEON

It flew low and alone
In the powder-blue, sunny sky,
A big black-gray pigeon
With a white head
And yellow eyes—
Flying low over the hurricane damaged resort
On the Bahamas island,
Over downed palm trees
By a long, aquamarine-colored swimming pool
Cyclone fences,
Closed gates…

SNOWBIRDS

The water is cold and choppy
Splashing white against the low, submerged rock
Further in, waves curl into thundering rolls by the
beach
Blowing mist over ochre sand…
Two mermaids rest there;
Green bodices and tails
With curled tassels on the forks,
The two sisters shiver on the beach
Hair blows, teeth chatter—
One lays on her back, knee up, watching her sister
Who sits nearby
With knee bent to one side
Leaning on one long, thin arm
Gazing intently at a map—
Twins, they are travelers too
Planning their next holiday;
A visit to a sunny shore for the winter—
Somewhere else!

*Snowbird: Someone who spends the winter in a warmer
climate

THE MERMAN

Who talks about the merman
If he indeed be?
We've never seen a merman
With the mermaids of the sea…

Much maligned, he is,
Ugly, some say too
Close eyes, a dumb look
Just to name a few…

If I were a merman
Angry, I would feel
I would ignore the mermaids
Till they made appeal

Till they put down their combs
In honor of their man
And begged for a kiss
Come get it if you can!

THE WAYWARD BUTTERFLY

Do you see that butterfly

Flying in the air so high?

How can it be

That something so small

Could fly across the river;

Should attempt it at all?

A PHILADELPHIA SWIMMING POOL

I looked out from the eighth floor
Of the W B Saunders building,
Down, past the park to Society Hill
By the Schuylkill river
To a swimming pool glimmering aqua-blue
No one using it…
I could see it clearly
But, something else caught my eye too;
A large, gray puddle left by the recent rain
On a rooftop
With a flock of pigeons around it
Wading and bathing…

A ROUGH SEA AT NIGHT

I slept on a cloud of white;
A soft and warm comforter—
While all along
Outside our balcony there was a storm

I was like a snowflake
Melting on quiet waters
While foam hissed behind the ship
And rolled forward to catch us in its embroiling grip—

THE BLUE FAIRY

Fairy of the evening-night
Blue-skinned fairy
With pointed, blue gossamer wings
Bathed in a golden light;
Shining gold particles within—
Like houses in the early morn
Muffled in blue snow,
Their windows lit-up golden before dawn
When the world is quiet and still—
Pretty fairy of the dark-hollow
Short, fuchsia hair in a cowlick
Fuchsia lips smiling
Green eyes smiling
Seeking to do good
To help someone
To give a kiss…
Come closer

RENDEZVOUS AT PUNTA DEL ESTE

Flat, tan sand
Darker tan where the water was—
Low waves roll in;
Blue colored, white edged
Under the blue sky
With little, white whirls in it,

It's where the lonely mermaid came to rest
On the Uruguay shore
On the open beach there
Punta Del Este—

It's where the lone dolphin came
Who tacked back and forth along the coast
Arching a black-gray fin above the sea now and then
In search of her…
On the Uruguay shore
On the open beach there
Punta Del Este—

It's where, at night
The crabs scuttled along the wet shoreline
To carry the news of the dolphin's arrival
To the waiting mermaid
On the Uruguay shore
On the open beach there
Punta Del Este—

It's where a falling star
Fell into the sea
Pointing out where the dolphin was
That the mermaid swam out to meet him
On the Uruguay shore
On the open beach there
Punta Del Este—

A PLAYFUL SNOW LEOPARD

He leaps high into the air
Whirling around to attack
That invisible enemy only a cat can see—
The sky so blue
The ground so snowy and cold
But, bright in the sunlight
His form so lithe
His fangs, large and yellow
His tail, puffy and long
His fur, white, mostly…
But tinged with orange
And covered with those black-gray spots
Leopards are famous for

THE BLACK MERMAID

She swam in gray, dark water
Frigid, cold and diffuse
Even at the surface
Where her green eyes glinted and glittered
Wide and anxious,
A brown skinned mermaid…

Foolish creature!
She had wasted time on the cloudy shore
Lying there wrapped in seaweed, counting the gulls
While the whale pod she waited for passed by;
Came looking for her
And left…
Now she was stranded
Not sure of which way to go…

She submerged in the black water
Becoming a gray blur herself only six feet under…
The floor was fifteen feet below
She went down to it
Resting on her elbows
To weep…

SHIP'S LOG

A ship's log
Is interesting to read
For a record is kept,
A careful record indeed…

The Gem's Log
Stated the absurd
It said a mermaid came aboard one day
In a little blurb

She dined on caviar
Cracked a lobster too
And sipped some champagne
While winking at the crew

She was a business woman,
Made quite a deal
Then she toured the ship
In a chair that they could wheel

She visited the captain,
Swept him quite away
And stayed aboard the ship
Till it reached the bay

There she gave her tail a slap
And dived into the green
That famous spotted tail;
The 'It" Mermaid was seen!

They say that she rules the Gem
Even from afar
For mermaids can steer a ship
From wherever they are…

THE OCTOPUS

Octo - because he has eight legs

Pus - because he isn't pretty

He slips and slides

And in crevices he hides

That's all to this ditty—

SHIPWRECK

Greenish sea whips and the moray eel,
Pea-soup green,

Swaying brown sea rods
The plumpest there has ever been,

And brain corals
Cluster in an ivory round

By the shipwreck
Slumbering peacefully on the ground—

Secrets that are kept
A hundredfold or more

Lie in the turquoise deep
On the coral floor

Where the black sea cucumber
And purple sea fans in a row

Guard the teakwood treasure
Hidden down below—

THE CHARDONNAY AD

The Irish mermaid…
Had long, wavy hair
Soft, gray eyes
Cute nose
And
A bright, yellow tail!

The Irish mermaid…
Had her portrait taken,
They used it
For Chardonnay
With
A flawless, yellow tail!

The Irish Mermaid…
Had, perhaps no tail
So she laughed
To see
There,
A slick, yellow tail!

LIGURIA

Opaque, turquoise-green sea
Reaching long, white fingers
Into the black sand;
Blue sky above
Gray, rocky cliffs watching—

*Liguria, Italy